Review of Selected Global Mineral Industries in 2011 and an Outlook to 2017

By W. David Menzie, Yadira Soto-Viruet, Omayra Bermúdez-Lugo, Philip M. Mobbs, Alberto Alexander Perez, Mowafa Taib, Susan Wacaster, and Staff

Open-File Report 2013–1091

U.S. Department of the Interior
U.S. Geological Survey

U.S. Department of the Interior
SALLY JEWELL, Secretary

U.S. Geological Survey
Suzette M. Kimball, Acting Director

U.S. Geological Survey, Reston, Virginia: 2013

For more information on the USGS—the Federal source for science about the Earth, its natural and living resources, natural hazards, and the environment—visit http://www.usgs.gov or call 1–888–ASK–USGS

For an overview of USGS information products, including maps, imagery, and publications, visit http://www.usgs.gov/pubprod

To order this and other USGS information products, visit http://store.usgs.gov

Suggested citation:
Menzie, W.D., Soto-Viruet, Yadira, Bermúdez-Lugo, Omayra, Mobbs, P.M., Perez, A.A., Taib, Mowafa, Wacaster, Susan, and Staff, 2013, Review of selected global mineral industries in 2011 and an outlook to 2017: U.S. Geological Survey Open-File Report 2013–1091, 33 p., http://pubs.usgs.gov/of/2013/1091.

Contents

Tables

Conversion Factors

Inch/Pound to SI

Multiply	By	To obtain
	Length	
mile (mi)	1.609	kilometer (km)
	Mass	
ounce, avoirdupois (oz)	28.35	gram (g)
ounce, troy	31.1035	gram (g)
pound, avoirdupois (lb)	0.4536	kilogram (kg)
ton, short (2,000 lb)	0.9072	megagram (Mg); metric ton (t)
ton, long (2,240 lb)	1.016	megagram (Mg); metric ton (t)
ton per day (ton/d)	0.9072	metric ton per day (t/d)
ton per year (ton/yr)	0.9072	metric ton per year (t/yr)

SI to Inch/Pound

Multiply	By	To obtain
	Length	
kilometer (km)	0.6214	mile (mi)
	Mass	
gram (g)	0.03527	ounce, avoirdupois (oz)
gram (g)	0.03215	ounce, troy
kilogram (kg)	2.205	pound avoirdupois (lb)
megagram (Mg); metric ton (t)	1.102	ton, short (2,000 lb)
megagram (Mg); metric ton (t)	0.9842	ton, long (2,240 lb)
metric ton per day (t/d)	1.102	ton per day (ton/d)
metric ton per year (t/yr)	1.102	ton per year (ton/yr)

Review of Selected Global Mineral Industries in 2011 and an Outlook to 2017

By W. David Menzie, Yadira Soto-Viruet, Omayra Bermúdez-Lugo, Philip M. Mobbs, Alberto Alexander Perez, Mowafa Taib, Susan Wacaster, and Staff

Introduction

This report reviews the world production of selected mineral commodities in 2011 and includes output projections (based on planned capacity expansions) through 2017. It also includes brief discussions of several issues that are of importance to the mineral sector, including the world economy, the availability of strategic minerals, significant company mergers and acquisitions in 2011, exploration investment made during the year, and the moves towards resource nationalization and expropriation of mineral assets by national Governments.

Economic Conditions

In 2011, the general condition of the world economy was that of a transition from a downturn to a slow recovery. This slow recovery, however, varied in magnitude from country to country and from industry to industry. There was no generalized pattern of recovery, and fears of a double-dip recession remained throughout the year. Slow growth is forecast for Europe, Japan, and the United States for 2012; however, there is a continuing possibility that the recovery could turn into a small decrease in world production of manufactured products.

China continued to be the world economy's primary engine of growth during 2011 as it has been since 2000, although the country's real growth rate as measured by the gross domestic product (GDP) dropped to 9.2 percent in 2011 from 10.4 percent in 2010. China remained the most significant single producer and a growing consumer of a wide variety of raw and processed minerals, including aluminum, antimony, barite, bismuth, cadmium, cement, coal, fluorspar, germanium, gold, graphite, indium, iron ore, lead, magnesium compounds and metal, mercury, molybdenum, rare earths, steel, strontium, tin, tungsten, and zinc. China's economy has grown at an average rate of 10.9 percent in the past 7 years (2005 to 2011). Since 2000, the Chinese Government has embarked on an ambitious program of public works projects, including making improvements to transportation and other basic infrastructure, which has required large amounts of mineral commodities. China also has become a major producer of manufactured goods and a principal commercial partner to the European Union, the United States, and much of the rest of the world (Embassy of the People's Republic of China in the United States of America, 2009; Davis, 2012a; U.S. Central Intelligence Agency, 2012).

Brazil's economy grew by only 2.8 percent in 2011 compared with 7.5 percent in 2010, or by one-half of the rate that the Government expected for 2011. It is likely that the European debt crisis and the slow economic recovery in the United States affected its growth; however, it also appears that Brazil, which has benefited from increased mineral exports in recent years, is suffering from a bout of Dutch disease—the phenomenon in which a boom in natural resource exports leads to currency appreciation, which in turn leads to a decrease in exports from other sectors of the economy. Higher interest rates in Brazil have attracted large amounts of foreign capital that, along with Brazil's mineral exports, have increased the value of the Brazilian currency. This, in turn, has made Brazil's exports of manufactured goods less competitive and is making imports more attractive, as in the case of its automotive industry. Mexican automobiles have become less expensive than those produced in Brazil, and auto imports from Mexico have increased. As a result, Brazil is seeking a treaty with Mexico to reduce Mexico's automobile exports into Brazil. Brazil is a resource-rich nation and, therefore, is sensitive to changes in patterns of mineral consumption in the world, especially that of China (one of its major trade partners), the United States, and the European Union. Any major changes in the consumption and production of these countries are likely to affect the Brazilian economy greatly. Also, Brazil will host the 2014 Soccer World Cup and the 2016 Summer Olympic Games. In anticipation of these events, major public works projects are being developed, which is increasing public spending and domestic demand for mineral resources. The Government is likely to incur new debt to finance these projects, which could present a problem if economic growth does not increase in the near future (Iliff and Jeffris, 2012; Lyons and Davis, 2012; Rolli, 2012).

The Indian economy grew at a rate of 7.8 percent in 2011 compared with 10.1 percent in 2010, and its services sector accounted for 55.6 percent of the GDP. The slower economic growth could make the Indian Government less likely to fulfill its promises of social spending and fuel subsidies that it expected to finance with revenues from the country's fast-growing economy. India's economic growth is limited by an insufficient supply of energy. Although the potential for increased industrial production in India remains positive, India, like Brazil, could be negatively affected by reduced consumption in Europe, Japan, and the United States (Lyons and Davis, 2012; Sharma and Bahree, 2012; Yep, 2012).

Economic growth in Russia is expected to decrease from more than 4 percent in 2011 to about 3.5 percent in 2012. Capital investment in Russia has slowed, and oil production is not expected to increase. Although some international firms are investing in Russia, others are selling their Russian investments. Disruptions in the delivery of natural gas from Russia to European markets continue to raise questions about the reliability of the supply of Russian oil to these markets (Iosebashvili, 2012; Kolyandr, 2012; Peaple, 2012; Torello and Robinson, 2012).

The sovereign debt crisis in Europe that was triggered by the potential default of Greece on its debt and the likely contagion that this would create on other markets, such as in Italy, Portugal, and Spain, created an environment of economic uncertainty in the European Union that affected both the ability and willingness of financial parties to invest in future projects in the mineral industry. This climate of investment restraint seems to have affected the development of long-term mining projects despite the increase in prices of many commodities.

Mineral Markets

Materials in this section of the report and in tables 1 through 15 come from Fong Sam and others, 2012; Mobbs and others, 2012; Perez and others, 2012: Wacaster and others, 2012: and Yager and others, 2012, unless otherwise indicated.

Metals

Bauxite.—In 2011, global bauxite production was about 220 million metric tons (Mt) compared with 216 Mt in 2010 (Bray, 2012b). Production increased in Guinea and China. Global production is projected to increase to 244 Mt by 2013, 279 Mt by 2015, and 312 Mt by 2017 (table 1). By 2017, Australia is expected to increase its bauxite production to 91 million metric tons per year (Mt/yr) owing to the expected capacity expansions at the Weipa and the South Embley Mines and the new capacities at the Aurukun Cape York and the Darling Range North projects. In Guinea, China Power Investment Corp. planned to develop a 12-Mt/yr bauxite mine at Boffa by 2015, and Global Alumina Corp. planned to construct a 10-Mt/yr bauxite mine at Sangaredi by 2017. The Porto Loko Mine in Sierra Leone is expected to be in operation by 2015 and to produce about 10 Mt/yr of bauxite. In Saudi Arabia, the Al Ba'itha Mine is expected to produce 3.5 Mt/yr by 2013. In Indonesia, state-owned Antam Tbk planned to increase bauxite production to 850,000 metric tons per year (t/yr) in 2010. Indonesia is expected to increase its production capacity by 19 Mt/yr between 2010 and 2017.

Aluminum.—World primary aluminum production in 2011 was estimated to have increased to 44.1 Mt in 2011, which was an 8 percent increase compared with output in 2010 (Bray, 2012a). China remained the leading producer with an estimated 18 Mt of primary production. Output increased as some existing facilities restarted production after shutting down in 2008 and 2009 and as new capacity was brought online, mainly in China and India. The London Metal Exchange Ltd. (LME) spot price of aluminum averaged $2,400 per metric ton in January 2011, but prices decreased to an average of about $2,000 per metric ton in December.

Global aluminum production, including primary and secondary materials, was about 51 Mt in 2010 (table 2), and production is projected to increase to 59 Mt by 2013, 63 Mt by 2015, and 66 Mt by 2017. In Canada, production is expected to be increased to 3.9 Mt/yr by 2017 owing to the expected increases in capacity at Rio Alcan's Kitimat smelter in British Columbia and new capacity at Rio Tinto Alcan's AP 60 plant in Quebec. Aluminum production in China is expected to increase by 6.8 Mt from 2010 to 2017 owing to several projects in development, which include 11 aluminum projects that were under construction and would have a total production of 1.12 Mt/yr, and an additional 10 aluminum projects that were in the feasibility stage and would have a total capacity of 1.4 Mt/yr.

Cobalt.—In 2010, global cobalt production was about 103,000 metric tons (t), and global output is projected to increase to 147,000 t by 2013, 167,000 t by 2015, and 179,000 t by 2017 (table 3). In Congo (Kinshasa), major expansions of capacity are planned at the Etoile, Kinsevere, Mutanda, Tenke Fungurume, KOV, KTO, Mukondo Mountain, and T17 Mines, which would increase the country's cobalt production by 55,000 t/yr by 2017. The Ambatovy Mine in Madagascar is expected to reach a capacity of 4,900 t/yr by 2013 and 5,600 t/yr by 2015. Expansion of Vale Nouvelle-Calédonie's Goro operation in New Caledonia is expected to increase the plant's capacity to 3,000 t/yr of cobalt by 2017.

Copper (Mine).—World mine output of copper is estimated to have been 16.1 Mt in 2011 (Edelstein, 2012). Chile remained the leading producer, accounting for about 34 percent of total world production. The LME spot price of copper metal averaged about $9,600 per metric ton in January 2011 but prices declined to an average of about $7,600 per metric ton in December based on concerns about European Union debt and changing economic policies in China (Davis, 2012a). High levels of Chinese imports were responsible for higher prices in the beginning of 2011.

Global copper production was about 16 Mt in 2010, and production is projected to increase to 18 Mt by 2013, 19 Mt by 2015, and 21 Mt by 2017 (table 4). In Congo (Kinshasa), major expansions of capacity are planned at the Etoile, KOV, KTO, Luiswishi, Mukondo Mountain, Ruashi, T17, and Tenke Fungurume Mines, which would increase the country's copper output to 990,000 t by 2017. In Australia, copper production is expected to increase by 380,000 t by 2017 owing to the planned expansions at the Copper Hill Project, the DeGrussa operation, the Kanmantoo Mine, and the Mount Elliot project. In Mongolia, the Nergui Mine, the Oyu Tolgoi mining complex, and the Tsagaan Survarga Mine are expected to come online between 2012 and 2015, which would increase the country's production capacity to 800,000 t/yr by 2017. In Chile, major expansions are planned at the Esperanza and Los Bronces Mines, and the country's copper production capacity is expected to increase by 581,000 t/yr by 2017. In Peru, new deposits are expected to be developed between 2013 and 2015, including Las Bambas and Los Chancas deposits in the Department of Apurimac and the Rio Blanco copper project in the Department of Piura. By 2012, major expansions are expected at the Antamina Mine in the Department of Ancash, Cerro Verde Mine in the Department of Arequipa, Cuajone Mine in the Department of Moquegua, and Toquepala Mine in the Department of Tacna.

Copper (Metal).—Global refined copper production was about 19 Mt in 2010, and it is projected to increase to 22 Mt by 2013 and 23 Mt by 2017 (table 5). Congo (Kinshasa)'s refined copper production is expected to increase to 899,000 t by 2017 owing to production increases at the Luilu, Luita, Ruashi, Tenke Fungurume, and Usoke Avenue solvent extraction and electrowinning (SX/EW) plants. Peru's production is expected to increase by about 156,000 t/yr from 2010 to 2017. New capacity is expected to come online between 2014 and 2015, including the Galeno copper project in the Department of Cajamarca, the Tia María copper project in the Department of Arequipa, and the Toromocho deposit in the Department of Junin. By 2012, major expansions are expected at the Southern Peru Copper Corp. refinery and smelter at Ilo in the Department of Moquegua.

Gold.—In 2011, gold production increased to about 2.7 million kilograms (Mkg) from 2.56 Mkg in 2010 (George, 2012). Market prices of gold and silver increased substantially, which reaffirmed their role as stores of value in times of economic uncertainty. The price of gold increased to $1,652 per troy ounce in December 2011 from $1,391 per troy ounce in December 2010 and $968 per troy ounce in March 2008, which was the month with the highest average gold prices between December 2001 and the worldwide financial crisis of 2008 to 2009. Increases in gold prices and production were mainly attributable to investment demand resulting from the worldwide financial crisis and continuing uncertainty in the global economy from debt problems confronting such countries as Greece, Ireland, Italy, Portugal, and Spain.

Global gold production is projected to increase to 2.8 Mkg by 2013, 3.1 Mkg by 2015, and 3.3 Mkg by 2017 (table 6). In Papua New Guinea, new capacity is expected to come online between 2013 and 2017, including at the Frieda River, Woodlark Island, and Yandera Mines. Papua New Guinea's gold production is expected to increase by about 68,000 kilograms (kg) from 2010 to 2017. In Australia, gold production is expected to increase by about 59,000 kg from 2010 to 2017 owing to the expected production increases at the Cosmo Deep Mine, the Deleton Mine, and the Tropicana joint-venture project. China's production is expected to increase by about 55,000 kilograms per year (kg/yr) from 2010 to 2017. In Mauritania, a major expansion was expected at the Tasiast Mine, which would increase the mine's production to 49,000 kg/yr by 2017.

Iron Ore.—In 2011, world output of iron contained in iron ore was estimated to have increased by about 8 percent to 1.4 billion metric tons (Gt) from 1.3 Gt in 2010 (Jorgenson, 2012). China remained the leading producer with about 25 percent of total production. Prices declined from January 2011 to December 2011, and leading iron ore producers reported reduced profits in the fourth quarter of the year. Iron ore prices are expected to remain low for at least the short term as substantial amounts of new capacity are brought online in 2012 and 2013 and as Chinese steel producers attempt to increase the amount of scrap used in steel production.

In 2010, global iron ore production was 1.32 Gt, and production is projected to increase to 1.52 Gt by 2013, 1.66 Gt by 2015, and 1.75 Gt by 2017 (table 7). In China, new capacity expansions are planned in Anhui, Liaoning, Sichuan, and Xianjiang Provinces, which would increase the country's production capacity to 430 Mt/yr by 2017. In Gabon, production is expected to begin at the Kango project by 2017 and to increase the country's production capacity to about 12.8 Mt/yr. In Guinea, new capacity is expected to come online at the Forecariah, Kalia, Mount Nimba, Simandou (Blocks 1 and 2), and Simandou (Blocks 3 and 4) Mines, which would increase the country's iron ore production capacity to almost 120 Mt/yr by 2017. In Senegal, the Faleme Mine is expected to come onstream by 2017 with a capacity of 4.3 Mt/yr. In Sierra Leone, 10.1 Mt/yr was expected to be added to the country's production capacity by 2017 owing to the opening of the Marampa and the Tonkolili Mines.

Steel.—Global crude steel production increased to 1.5 Gt in 2011 from about 1.4 Gt in 2010 (Fenton, 2012). It is projected to continue to increase to 1.6 Gt by 2013, 1.7 Gt by 2015, and more than 1.7 Gt by 2017 (table 8). In China, capacity expansions are planned in Guangdong, Guangxi, and Hebei Provinces, which would increase the country's production to 780 Mt/yr of crude steel by 2017. Major expansions of capacity are planned in Liaoning Province and Jilin Province, with an expected increase in steel production capacity of 30 Mt/yr and 10 Mt/yr, respectively. Brazil's crude steel production capacity is expected to increase to about 40 Mt/yr by 2017.

Palladium.—In 2011, global palladium production was about 207,000 kg (Loferski, 2012). It is projected to increase to 220,000 kg by 2013, 230,000 kg by 2015 and 236,000 kg by 2017 (table 9). In South Africa, palladium production is projected to increase by about 26,000 kg from 2010 to 2017 owing to the opening of the Booysedal, Kalahari, Mareesbusg, Rooderport, and Styldrift Mines, and the Western Bushveld Joint Venture. Major expansions of capacity are expected at the Everest, Bokoni, Crocodile River, Eland, Impala, Marikana, Marula, Nkomati, Pilanesburg, and Two Rivers Mines. Palladium production is expected to increase in Canada and Zimbabwe to 19,000 kg/yr and 11,000 kg/yr, respectively, by 2017.

Platinum.—In 2011, global platinum production was about 192,000 kg (Loferski, 2012). It is projected to increase to 226,000 kg by 2013, 241,000 kg by 2015 and 248,000 kg by 2017 (table 10). In South Africa, new capacity is expected to come online at the Booysedal, Kalahari, Mareesbusg, Rooderport, and Styldrift Mines and the Western Bushveld Joint Venture. Major expansions of capacity are also expected at the Everest, Bokoni, Crocodile River, Eland, Impala, Marikana, Marula, Nkomati, Pilanesburg, and Two Rivers Mines, which would increase the country's annual capacity to 193,000 kg by 2017.

Tin (Mine).—In 2011, global mine production of tin was about 253,000 t (Carlin, 2012). It is projected to increase to 261,000 t by 2013, to decrease to 256,000 t by 2015, and to remain at that level through 2017 (table 11). In Egypt, new capacity is planned to come online at the Abu Dababb tin and tantalum mine, which is expected to begin operation by 2013 and to produce about 1,530 t/yr of tin.

Tin (Metal).—In 2010, global production of refined tin was about 321,000 t. It is projected to increase to 343,000 t by 2013, 362,000 t by 2015, and 385,000 t by 2017 (table 12). In China, annual production capacity is expected to increase to 180,000 t/yr of refined metal by 2017. In Indonesia, the Yunnan Tin Co. Ltd. planned to develop a tin smelter, which would increase the country's production capacity to 55,000 t/yr by 2017. In Thailand, production capacity is expected to increase to 30,000 t/yr by 2017.

Industrial Minerals

Diamond.—In 2010, global diamond production (gem and industrial) was about 127 million carats. It is projected to increase to 137 million carats by 2013, 140 million carats by 2015, and 143 million carats by 2017 (table 13). The reopening of the Damtshaa Mine and the opening of new capacities at the AK6, BK11, and Gopa Mines in Botswana would increase the country's production capacity to about 28 million carats by 2013. In Canada, diamond production is expected to increase to 16 million carats by 2017 owing to the reopening of the Jericho Mine and several early-stage projects. Diamond production is expected to increase in Congo (Kinshasa) and Zimbabwe by 2.7 million carats and 1.6 million carats, respectively, from 2010 to 2017.

Fertilizer Minerals (Nitrogen, Phosphate Rock, and Potash).—According to the Food and Agriculture Organization of the United Nations (FAO), consumption of fertilizer nutrients has been increasing since 2010, and it is expected to continue to increase through 2015. FAO projected increases in demand for total fertilizer nutrients from 2011 to 2015, including an increase of 1.7 percent for nitrogen, 1.9 percent for phosphate, and 3.1 percent for potash. As fertilizer consumption increases, food prices are also expected to increase. The food price index increased to 233 in 2011 compared with an index of 200 in 2008. Increased use of biofuels is also contributing to the increased price of foods, and biofuels production is expected to increase because of the high price of crude oil. About 40 percent of the U.S. corn crop was used for production of biofuels in 2011. Increases in world population, the use of biofuels, and food prices are expected to encourage farmers to apply more fertilizer to achieve higher yields. Global production of ammonia, diammonium phosphate (DAP), phosphate rock, phosphoric acid, potash, and sulfur increased by 5 percent from 2005 to 2011 (Fathallah, 2012).

According to the International Fertilizer Association, in 2011 world production of phosphate rock was 191 Mt; ammonia, 163 Mt; urea, 155 Mt; potash, 56 Mt; sulfur, 51 Mt; phosphoric acid, 42 Mt; and DAP, 33 Mt. China was the world's leading producer of urea and accounted for 30 percent of global production (Apodaca, 2012; Heffer and Prud'homme, 2012; Jasinski, 2012a, b).

China remained the leading producer of phosphate rock in 2011 and accounted for about 38 percent of the world's production (Jasinski, 2012a). Morocco, which was the world's leading exporter of phosphate rock, entered into a joint-venture agreement with Yara International ASA of Norway in to build a new port facility in Rio Grande, Brazil, where Yara would process imported phosphate rock from Morocco into fertilizer and other products. New phosphate rock suppliers came online, including in Peru in 2010 and Saudi Arabia and Kazakhstan in 2011. India was a major market for imported fertilizer in 2011; it imported 100 percent of its potash and 75 percent of its phosphate requirements. Indian companies have been creating joint ventures with potash and phosphate rock producers in Australia, Jordan, Morocco, Peru, and the United States to secure supplies of these commodities.

Potash was the most traded fertilizer component. Production was concentrated in 10 countries (Canada, Russia, Belarus, Germany, China, Israel, Jordan, the United States, Chile, and the United Kingdom, in descending order of production). Consumption (70 percent) took place in six countries (Brazil, China, India, Indonesia, Malaysia, and the United States) (Jasinski, 2012b). New plants and expansions at existing facilities are expected to increase the production for potash in the next few years in Argentina, Belarus, Brazil, Canada, China, Congo (Brazzaville), and the United Kingdom.

Lithium.—In 2010, global lithium production was about 28,000 t. It is projected to increase to about 35,000 t by 2013, 41,000 t by 2015, and to remain at that level to 2017 (table 14). In Australia, a major expansion of processing capacity is planned at Greenbushes by 2017. In Canada, the Quebec Lithium Project was expected to begin operation by 2013 and to produce about 3,000 t/yr of lithium by 2017. By 2017, lithium production capacity in Brazil is expected to increase to about 510 t/yr.

Mineral Fuels and Related Materials

Coal.—In 2011, world coal production increased to about 7.7 Gt from 7.3 Gt in 2010. At yearend 2011, the total estimated proven global reserves of coal was estimated to be about 861 Gt. Europe and Eurasia had the largest reserves (35.4 percent of the world total) led by Russia (18.2 percent of the world total), followed by the Asia and the Pacific region (30.9 percent), North America (28.5 percent), the Middle East and Africa (3.8 percent), and South America and Central America (1.5 percent) (BP p.l.c., 2012, p. 30, 32).

From 2000 through 2010, growth in global energy demand was satisfied primarily by coal supplies. Global coal demand is expected to increase to about 600,000 metric tons per day by 2016, despite prices that have been increasing sharply and fluctuating since about 2004. Although the prices of coking coal and steam coal have increased, the price for coking coal has been increasing more rapidly since about 2005. China is expected to have the largest increase in coal production. The country generates about 70 percent of its electricity from coal (Houssin, 2012).

According to the International Energy Agency, coal will make a substantial contribution to the global energy mix to 2016. The global supply of, demand for, investment in, and trade of coal will depend upon such uncertainties as the level of economic activity, port capacities, mining capacities, Chinese growth and trade policies, supply shocks, and long-term changes in the nature and rate of decarbonization (Houssin, 2012).

Global coal production is projected to increase to 7.7 Gt by 2013, 8.0 Gt by 2015, and 8.3 Gt by 2017 (table 15). In Australia, major expansions of capacity are planned at the Hunter Valley and Ulan West Coal Mines in the State of New South Wales, which would increase the country's production capacity to 560 Mt/yr. In China, Shenhua Coal Group planned to develop the Buertai Coal Mine in Nei Mogol Autonomous Region with a designed capacity of 20 Mt/yr of coal. The Government of China expected to increase coal production in Shanxi Province to 750 Mt/yr by 2012.

Natural Gas.—According to the International Energy Agency, global resources of natural gas are estimated to exceed 250 times the production volume of 2011. The Eastern Europe and Eurasia region had the greatest quantity of proven reserves and other recoverable conventional gas (nearly 140 trillion cubic meters) followed by the Middle East (about 120 trillion cubic meters). Other regions—which included Africa, Asia and the Pacific, Western Europe, Latin America, and North America—were each reported to have between about 20 trillion cubic meters and 40 trillion cubic meters in proven reserves and other recoverable conventional gas. In terms of recoverable unconventional gas resources, the Eastern Europe and Eurasia region and the North America region were each reported to have between 90 trillion cubic meters and 100 trillion cubic meters followed by the Asia and the Pacific region, about 80 trillion cubic meters; Latin America, about 50 trillion cubic meters; Africa, about 40 trillion cubic meters; and Western Europe and the Middle East, about 20 trillion cubic meters each (Houssin, 2012; van der Hoeven, 2012).

According to BP p.l.c., global production of natural gas in 2011 was about 3.3 trillion cubic meters. Europe and Eurasia accounted for about 32 percent of the total, followed by Russia with about 18 percent of the world total. Europe and Eurasia was followed by North America (26 percent), the Asia and the Pacific region (about 15 percent), the Middle East (about 14 percent), Africa (about 6 percent), and Central America and South America (5 percent). Natural gas trade grew by 10.1 percent in 2010 because of a 22.6 percent increase in liquefied natural gas (LNG) shipments. LNG accounted for 30.5 percent of the global gas trade; the Middle East was the leading exporting region. Qatar was the world's leading LNG supplier, and its exports increased by 53.2 percent from those in 2009. Pipeline shipments increased by 5.4 percent in 2010 and were led by Russia. Europe and Eurasia accounted for about two-thirds of global trade in natural gas by pipeline (BP p.l.c., 2012; Global LNG Ltd., 2012).

In 2011, interest in Europe's shale gas reserves increased. Despite controversy concerning the process by which it is produced, unconventional shale gas has emerged as an important part of the active energy portfolio in North America and is a potentially important source of natural gas around the world as well. In Europe, Exxon Mobil Corp. of the United States explored for shale gas in Poland and Germany. Poland was expected to release an official shale gas estimate of about 1 trillion cubic meters in 2012, which is only about one-fifth of what had been previously estimated by other sources. Poland still planned to develop the shale gas to reduce its dependency on domestically produced coal and on gas imports. Poland granted more than 100 shale-gas exploration licenses, but ExxonMobil reported that it had not yet found commercial quantities of gas. The company reported that it could be 5 years before European shale production comes online and stated that Germany was likely to be the first European shale gas producer, provided Germany does not ban the hydraulic fracturing process that is required to recover that gas. Some very large shale gas finds have been reported elsewhere in Europe but little or no exploratory drilling has been conducted (Bergin, 2012; Thomson Reuters, 2012c).

The Chinese Government released a plan in early 2012 announcing its intention to begin producing large volumes of shale gas, and that production was expected to reach 6.5 billion cubic meters in 2015 and at least 10 times that by 2020. Large-scale exploration, however, had not yet begun in the country when the report was released, but the Government urged Chinese companies to work with foreign entities with expertise in finding and exploiting unconventional natural gas resources. China's Ministry of Land and Resources reported that the country has about 25 trillion cubic meters of potentially recoverable shale gas reserves, and the U.S. Energy Information Administration estimated Chinese reserves to be about 36 trillion cubic meters (Chen, 2012).

OAO Gazprom of Russia, which was the world's leading natural gas exporter, planned to supply LNG to India starting in 2016, but this is also the year that the United States is expected to begin exporting shale gas as record production in North America has driven down U.S. prices of this commodity. Such exports could compete with Russian exports to Asian gas markets. Asia accounts for more than 60 percent of global demand for LNG, and the region imported about 178 billion cubic meters in 2010. GAIL India Ltd., which was India's leading gas supplier, was the first Asian company to buy U.S. natural gas in 2011 when it signed a 20-year deal with Cheniere Energy Partners LP, which planned to supply 3.5 Mt/yr starting in 2017. Gazprom already had tentative long-term supply agreements in 2011 with GAIL and several other companies, but the Russian supplier ties the price in long-term contracts to the price of oil. Some European customers have resisted such pricing, and China has refused to pay Russia prices for natural gas that are equivalent to those it charges European customers (Shiryaevskaya, 2012).

In 2011, Japan's utility companies consumed a record 5 Mt of LNG compared with 3.47 Mt in 2010, as the country was forced to offset the decline in nuclear power generation in the aftermath of the Fukushima Daiichi Nuclear Power Plant accident. The accident resulted in a record 12.1 percent decrease in electricity production compared with that of 2010. Inpex Corp. of Japan, which was the country's top oil and gas developer, announced in early 2012 that it would buy a 15.55 percent stake in the *Prelude* floating LNG project in Australia from Royal Dutch Shell plc of the Netherlands. The *Prelude* project was expected to be the first floating LNG project to come online, although several other projects were expected to come online by the end of the decade (Maeda, 2011; Negishi and Tsukimori, 2012).

Uranium.—As a result of Japan's Fukushima Daiichi nuclear accident that occurred on March 11, 2011, uncertainty about the role of nuclear power increased significantly and led to policy changes, particularly in Europe where Germany voted to end nuclear power generation by 2022. Around the world, the event heightened the awareness of and debate about nuclear energy. In June 2012, Japan restarted its first nuclear reactor No. 3 at the Oi complex, which is operated by Kansai Electric Power Co. The country planned to restart its second reactor (No. 4), which is located 370 kilometers west of Tokyo, in July 2012. After the earthquake and the tsunami, 50 nuclear reactors were taken offline for maintenance and tests; however, no further details were available as to when the other reactors would be restarted. Prior to the Fukushima Daiichi accident, the price of uranium had been as high as $73 per pound ($161,000 per metric ton); at the time of the accident, it was $66 per pound ($145,000 per metric ton). By yearend 2011, the price had fallen to $52 per pound ($115,000 per metric ton). Nevertheless, some countries, including China, India, the Republic of Korea, and Russia, reportedly remained committed to ambitious nuclear programs similar to those that were adopted in the 1970s when the first global oil shock resulted in nuclear power expansion in France, Japan, and the United States. The Fukushima accident led some countries, including the United States, to comprehensively review their nuclear power generation operations for safety, focusing primarily on backup power systems that would provide protection against extreme external events. As of mid- to late-2011, there were 65 reactors under construction worldwide, including 5 in the Republic of Korea, which already had 21 connected to the grid; 2 in Japan, which had 50 connected to the grid at the time of the accident; and 1 in the United States, which has 104 reactors connected to the power grid. Canada had 17 reactors connected to its power grid but none under construction. Canada's deuterium reactors supply about 15 percent of the country's electricity. France, which has 58 nuclear reactors, obtains more than 75 percent of its electricity from nuclear energy; in fact, it is the largest net exporter of electricity because of its low cost of generation. France uses about 12,000 t of uranium oxide concentrate (10,500 t of uranium) per year, of which 4,500 t comes from Canada's Areva reactor, and 3,200 t comes from Niger. About 17 percent of France's electricity is from recycled nuclear fuel (Natural Resources Canada, 2009; Mining Journal, 2011a, b; Organisation for Economic Co-operation and Development, 2011; Gordon, 2012; Maeda, 2012a, b; World Nuclear Association, 2012).

Strategic Minerals

There has been a great deal of concern about the availability of minerals needed for industrial production in Europe, Japan, and the United States in recent years. Much of the concern has crystallized around rare-earth elements, which have received very broad attention in both the media and professional circles. China is rich in rare-earth resources, accounting for about 50 percent of the world's total rare-earth resources. In addition to raw rare-earth minerals, China produces a variety of processed products, including rare-earth metals and chemicals. Since the 1990s, China has become the leading rare-earth-element producing country in the world, accounting for more than 90 percent of the world's total output. Over the past decade, such countries as France, Italy, Japan, and the United States have depended upon rare-earth elements exported from China. Before 2000, China's rare-earth production exceeded domestic demand; at that time, suppliers in China exported significant amounts of rare-earth products to overseas markets. In 2000, China produced 73,000 t of mined rare-earth elements (rare-earth oxide equivalent) and consumed about 19,000 t. From 1990 to 2000, China exported unprocessed rare-earth elements (Cordier, 2012; Menzie, 2012).

In the past 10 years, however, Chinese domestic demand for rare-earth elements increased sharply. The country's rare-earth production increased to more than 120,000 t; further, domestic consumption of rare-earth elements increased to 87,000 t by 2010. At the same time, the Chinese Government issued measures calling for restricted production, and the Government further restricted exportation of rare-earth elements. China no longer exports unprocessed rare-earth elements. In addition, the rare-earth export quota decreased to about 30,000 t in 2010 from 47,000 t in 2000. Chinese statistics indicate that the country's rare-earth production has remained at 120,000 t during the past several years (Menzie, 2012).

China's restriction of rare-earth exports has significantly affected the downstream sectors of other countries, especially France, Italy, and Japan, which do not have identified rare-earth resources. In the United States, the reopening of the Mountain Pass Mine in California in late 2011 is expected to reduce U.S. demand for processed rare earths from China in the coming years. In addition, Lynas Corp. Ltd. of Australia completed construction of its Mount Weld Mine in Western Australia in 2010. These two mines can supply a total of about 30,000 t of mined rare-earth elements beginning in 2012 and will reduce the demand for Chinese-produced rare-earth elements. Mountain Pass and Mount Weld, however, contain mainly light rare earths (lanthanum, cerium, praseodymium, neodymium, samarium, and europium). Many electronic products require heavy rare earths (gadolinium, terbium, dysprosium, holmium, erbium, thulium, ytterbium, and lutetium) to perform more efficiently. Currently, China is the only country that can supply significant amounts of both light and heavy rare-earth products. At least for the next several years, China will continue to be the major supplier of heavy rare-earth elements (Menzie, 2012).

The concerns are not, however, limited to rare-earth elements and supplies of raw minerals. The issue extends across mineral commodities and throughout the supply chain of manufactured goods. Since the 2008 publication of two reports by the National Research Council (Minerals, Critical Minerals, and the U.S. Economy) and the National Academy of Engineering (Managing Materials for a Twenty-First Century Military), it has become apparent that the Department of Defense and major U.S. corporations, such as General Electric Co., were unaware of the degree to which they depended on numerous minerals and mineral materials. Perhaps this should not be surprising as they typically do not buy raw materials, but mainly purchase component parts or integrated systems. Events such as the Japan earthquake of 2010 have served to highlight how supply chains can be interrupted with consequent effects across a variety of economic actors, some gaining and others losing as a result of the disruption (National Research Council, 2008a, b; Menzie, 2012).

Mergers and Acquisitions

The higher-than-average number of mergers and acquisitions (M&As) in the mining sector in 2011 is attributable to several factors, including low interest rates, increased cash reserves of many large- and medium-sized mining companies, and the availability of a number of prospect-rich exploration and mining companies. Some companies also engaged in share repurchase programs; BHP Billiton completed a $10 billion buyback program that it had resumed in late 2010 (MacDonald, 2011).

The year 2011 was not only the second busiest year in history in terms of the number of proposed M&As in the mining sector but it was the one with the fewest proposed mining M&As cancelled since 2004. A total of 2,605 mining M&A deals with a reported value of $149 billion were disclosed during the year. These deals represented a 33 percent increase in the value of announced mining M&A transactions compared with that of 2010; the average value of these deals increased by 50 percent to $105 million from $70 million during 2010. M&A transactions in the mining sector that were valued at less than $100 million accounted for 1,355 deals, although the megadeals (greater than $1 billion) received the most press coverage. Australia, Canada, and the United States held a 57 percent share of all 2011 mining acquisitions worldwide, and Canada held a 30 percent share of the M&A market. Also, Australia, Canada, and the United States accounted for 53 percent of the year's acquisition value; Australia held the top position with a 22 percent share of the market, and the United States displaced China by holding a 17 percent market share (PricewaterhouseCoopers LLP, 2012, p. 6–10).

China and Russia together accounted for 16 percent of the global mining deals by value and 11 percent by volume. Among the world's developing economies, China represented about one-half of the growth in the market and its buying volume increased by about 40 percent from the world's 2006 market peak volumes and 300 percent from 2006 market peak values. Other noticeable players in the developing economies were India-based buyers, which took part in 26 acquisitions worth $1.6 billion; Indonesia-based buyers, which accounted for $1.3 billion worth of mining buys; and Republic of Korea-based buyers, which accounted for $2.6 billion worth of buys (PricewaterhouseCoopers LLP, 2012, p. 10–11).

On a country-by-country basis, financial analysts observed a "geographic clustering" in terms of buyers favoring and participating in projects located in their own markets. This was notable both for developed as well as developing economies. About 64 percent of Australian-led acquisitions involved projects in Australia; 61 percent of Canadian-led acquisitions involved projects in Canada; and 60 percent of United States-led acquisitions involved projects in the United States. Likewise, in the non-Western developing economies, 100 percent of Mexican-led acquisitions involved projects in Mexico; 90 percent of Russian-led acquisitions involved projects in Russia; 75 percent of Brazilian-led acquisitions involved projects in Brazil, and 64 percent of Chinese-led acquisitions involved projects in mainland China. About 44 percent of the deals announced by Western-based companies outside of their own territory involved projects in Latin America. The second most popular destination for overseas M&A investments was Africa (PricewaterhouseCoopers LLP, 2012, p. 10–14).

The five key mineral commodities that dominated global M&A investments were coal, copper, gold, iron ore, and niobium. These commodities represented about 81 percent of the aggregate values of firms that were the object of mergers or acquisitions; 41 percent of copper transactions (by value) were for targets in China, Congo (Kinshasa), Mongolia, Namibia, and Zambia. Although the majority of transactions involving iron ore took place in Australia, Canada, and China, significant acquisitions involving iron ore also took place in Afghanistan, Cameroon, Congo (Brazzaville), and Russia. In terms of volume, copper, gold, iron ore, silver, and uranium represented 57 percent of all M&A activity. Gold dominated investments (by volume) accounted for 31 percent of M&A deals (PricewaterhouseCoopers LLP, 2012, p. 16). In the fuels sector, a total of 1,322 oil and gas M&A transactions were announced in 2011, which was an increase of more than 5 percent from that of 2010 (Deloitte Development LLC, 2011).

Significant mergers or acquisitions in the mineral sector during 2011 included the following:

- $8.5 billion (coal)—Virginia-based Alpha Natural Resources, Inc. merged with Virginia-based Massey Energy Co. The merger would have Alpha in control of the second ranked coal reserve base in the United States (Alpha Natural Resources, Inc., 2011).
- $7.5 billion (copper)—In July, Canadian company Barrick Gold Corp. acquired 100 percent of the issued and outstanding common shares of Equinox Minerals Ltd. of Canada for $7.482 billion. Equinox's assets included the operating Lumwana copper mine in Zambia and the Jabal Sayid copper project in Saudi Arabia, which is expected to enter production in 2012 (Barrick Gold Corp., 2011; 2012, p. 17–18; Donville, 2011; Nicholson, 2011).
- $5.4 billion (copper)—Mitsubishi Corp.of Japan acquired 24.5 percent of Anglo American Sur S.A. of Chile, which holds a significant portfolio of copper assets in Chile, including Los Bronces Mine, El Soldado Mine, the Chagres smelter, and a number of other exploration properties (Mitsubishi Corp., 2011).
- $5.2 billion (bauxite and aluminum)—Norsk Hydro ASA of Norway acquired significant Brazilian bauxite and alumina assets from Companhia Vale do Rio Doce (Vale) of Brazil. Norsk Hydro obtained full control and ownership of the Paragominas bauxite mine, a 91 percent share in the Alunorte alumina refinery, an 81 percent share in the CAP alumina refinery, and a 51 percent share in the Albras aluminum plant, among other assets (Norsk Hydro ASA, 2011).
- $4.8 billion (iron ore)—In May, Ohio-based Cliffs Natural Resources Inc. acquired Consolidated Thompson Iron Mines Ltd. of Canada. Following the merger, Cliffs is expected to become one of the leading mining and natural resources companies in North America and to have significant exposure to Asian markets. Cliffs will control 10 iron ore facilities, 6 coal mines, and a prefeasibility chromite-development project in Australia, North America, and South America (Cliffs Natural Resources Inc., 2011a; 2011b, p. 7; 2011c, p. 6).

- $4.8 billion (coal)—Australian company Whitehaven Coal Ltd. agreed to merge with Aston Resources Ltd. in December 2011. The merger would create Australia's leading independent coal company. Whitehaven was also to acquire Boardwalk Resources Ltd. for about $86 million. Boardwalk held interests in coal exploration assets across New South Wales and Queensland, Australia (Mishkin, 2011; Whitehaven Coal Ltd., 2012).
- $4.7 billion (coal)—In December, Missouri-based Peabody Energy Inc. completed the acquisition of all outstanding shares in Macarthur Coal Ltd. of Australia. Macarthur's assets included majority interest in the Coppabella, Middlemont, and Moorvale Mines in Australia in addition to a number of mine development and infrastructure projects, which were expected to become operational between 2012 and 2014 (Peabody Energy Inc., 2011).
- $2.84 billion (copper)—In December, KGHM Polska Miedz S.A. of Poland signed a binding conditional agreement with Canadian company Quadra FNX Mining Ltd. under which KGHM would acquire 100 percent of the shares of Quadra FNX. Quadra mined copper, nickel, gold, platinum, and palladium from the Carlota and Robinson Mines in the United States; the Franke Mine in Chile; and the McCreedy West, Levack, and Podolsky Mines in Canada (KGHM Polska Miedz S.A., 2012, p. 20).
- $2.5 billion (gold)—In December, Eldorado Gold Corp. of Canada agreed to acquire all the outstanding common shares of European Goldfields Ltd. of Canada. European Goldfields held a 95 percent interest in Greece's Stratoni Mine, a 95 percent interest in the Skouries and Olympias projects, also in Greece, and an 80.1 percent interest in the Certej project in Romania. European gold reserves are estimated to be 286,000 kg (Eldorado Gold Corp., 2012, p. 2).
- $2.3 billion (gold)—Colorado-based Newmont Mining Corp. acquired all the outstanding common shares of Fronteer Gold Inc. of Canada in April. Fronteer held interest in three gold projects in the State of Nevada, with an estimated measured, indicated, and inferred resource of about 177,000 kg of gold (Newmont Mining Corp., 2011, p. 26–27).

Exploration

In 2011, according to Engineering and Mining Journal's annual survey of global mining investment, the Raw Materials Group (RMG) of Sweden estimated that the total value of announced investment in the global mining industry (this included coverage of precious, base, and ferrous metals; ferroalloys; and coal) increased by 20 percent to $676 billion compared with that of 2010. Based upon RMG criteria, Australia maintained its position as the leading nation for total mining investment in 2011 followed by Canada (Ericsson and Larsson, 2012).

Despite the recorded increase in global mining investments, the number of projects that had reached the feasibility stage declined for a second consecutive year, which was in part attributable to a sharp decline in exploration in 2009 (exploration spending reached a low of $8.4 billion in 2009) as a result of the global economic downturn of 2008 to 2009. Boart Longyear of the United States, which is one of the world's largest mineral exploration drilling companies, reported a record year in 2011, with a 37 percent increase in revenue to $2 billion compared with that of 2010. Demand for the company's drilling services was focused mostly in Latin America and Africa, reflecting the demand for gold and copper from those regions. The company also reported that its revenue had decreased by about 50 percent in 2009 when many junior exploration companies closed and the major companies, which represented 80 percent of its revenue, scaled back their exploration programs. Boart Longyear, however, expected about 14 percent growth in revenues in 2012, primarily as a result of the activities in Africa and Latin America that contributed to record revenues in 2011 (Metals Economics Group, 2011; Ericsson and Larsson, 2012; Topf, 2012).

Based on its survey of planned nonfuel and nonferrous exploration spending (which included coverage of precious and base metals, as well as lithium, niobium, phosphate, potash, rare-earth elements, tantalum, and uranium), the Metals Economics Group (MEG) of Canada reported that global exploration spending increased by about 50 percent in 2011 to $18.2 billion. According to the MEG's criteria, Latin America was the leading region for planned mineral commodity exploration budgets in 2011, with 26 percent of the total, followed by Canada (18 percent), Africa (15 percent), Australia (12 percent), the United States (8 percent), the Pacific region (not including Australia) and Southeast Asia (6 percent), and the rest of the world, including China and Russia (15 percent) (Els, 2011; Metals Economics Group, 2011).

According to the MEG, Mexico, which invested $1 billion in exploration in 2011, was Latin America's leading country in terms of global exploration spending in 2011, accounting for 6 percent of the total; it was followed by Chile (5 percent), Peru (4 percent), Brazil (3 percent), and Argentina and Colombia (2 percent each). The group reported that Mexico's exploration spending had grown faster than the world average since 2003 and that its growth was attributed to increased spending by Canadian junior exploration companies. According to data compiled by the U.S. Geological Survey (USGS), Mexico led the region in terms of the number of exploration sites, followed by Peru, Brazil, Argentina, Chile, and Colombia (Jamasmie, 2012a, b; Wilburn and others, 2012).

According to Natural Resources Canada, Canada's exploration and deposit appraisal expenditures by junior and senior companies (including field work, overhead costs, engineering, economic and feasibility studies, environmental work, and land access costs) increased by 42 percent in 2011 compared with those of 2010. Those investments were about evenly distributed between junior and senior companies in 2011 that spent $1.9 billion and $1.8 billion, respectively, reflecting increases of about 62 percent by senior companies and 26 percent by junior companies compared with 2010 expenditures. Precious metals exploration led expenditures with about $1.9 billion, followed by diamond (about $980 million); base metals (about $690 million); other metals, coal, and nonmetals (about $590 million); iron ore (about $290 million); and uranium (about $200 million) (Natural Resources Canada, 2012a, b).

In 2011, the African exploration budget as determined by the MEG increased by about 70 percent compared with that of 2010. Based on data compiled by the USGS, gold and silver exploration projects accounted for about one-half of the known African exploration projects followed by base metals (10 percent), uranium (9 percent), iron ore (7 percent), and diamond and platinum-group metals (6 percent each). The International Finance Corp. (IFC) announced that it planned to invest $300 million in mining during the next 3 years in mining companies that operated in Africa. The IFC planned to direct part of that sum to equity investments with junior mining companies seeking financing for exploration projects and feasibility studies, and another portion toward debt investments in mining projects at other stages of development. About 230 Australian companies owned about 650 mining projects in 43 countries and territories of Africa, accounting for more than 40 percent of Australia's overseas mining projects (Davenport, 2011; Metals Economics Group, 2011; Swanepoel, 2011; Wilburn and others, 2012).

According to the Australian mineral exploration review 2011, spending on mineral exploration by Australian companies increased by 32 percent to about $2.3 billion in fiscal year 2011 compared with that of fiscal year 2010. Exploration spending increased for most commodities, including coal, cobalt, copper, gold, iron ore, lead, nickel, silver, uranium, and zinc. Decreased exploration spending was recorded for diamond and mineral sands. Exploration for iron ore received the most spending, accounting for about $680 million, or 29 percent of the total, followed by gold, which accounted for about $670 million, or about 28 percent of the total exploration budget of Australian companies (Senior and Huleatt, 2012, p. 1).

According to the MEG, exploration spending in the Pacific region (not including Australia) and Southeast Asia increased by about 39 percent in 2011 to about $1 billion compared with that of 2010. Indonesia, Papua New Guinea, and the Philippines combined accounted for about 80 percent of that exploration budget. In 2011, China, which received almost one-half of its iron ore imports from Australia, had begun to invest about $4.5 billion during 5 years to explore for minerals in 21 Provinces primarily to reduce its volume of iron ore imports. Five Chinese iron ore deposits were reported to hold up to 5 Gt of ore, but several deposits had low-grade ore. In early 2012, China was purchasing iron ore for about $135 per metric ton that cost only about $25 per metric ton to mine in Australia. China also had large petroleum and natural gas discoveries, including what was reported to be 1.37 Gt of proven reserves (a 21 percent increase compared with those of 2010) and about 770 billion cubic meters of proven natural gas reserves (an increase of 29.6 percent compared with those of 2010) (Kosich, 2010; Metals Economics Group, 2011; Thomson Reuters, 2012a, b).

Resource Nationalization

In 2011, resource nationalization was at the forefront of global issues affecting the mining sector. A report by Ernst & Young (2011) titled Business Risks Facing Mining and Metals 2011–2012 identified resource nationalism as the leading risk affecting businesses worldwide. Resource nationalization and expropriation of mineral assets, however, were more of a threat (with a few exceptions) than a fact in 2011. Milder forms of resource nationalization were manifested through Government initiatives aimed at obtaining a greater share of mining profits through changes in the fiscal environment by establishing higher taxes and royalties. Analysts estimated that between 2010 and 2011, at least 25 countries increased or announced intentions to increase their Government's participation in mining projects by imposing higher taxes or royalties. The rapid rebound of mineral commodity prices following the financial crises of 2008 to 2009 was considered one of the primary reasons for this trend, particularly in developing economies. In 2011, many countries—including Bolivia, Chile, China, Ghana, Guinea, Indonesia, Mongolia, Namibia, Nigeria, Panama, Peru, South Africa, Tanzania, Venezuela, Zambia, and Zimbabwe—either sought to obtain a greater participation in mining projects or demanded reviews and possible renegotiation of mining contracts, or increased royalties, mining taxes, or profit sharing. Some examples of the proposed actions were as follows:

- The Australian Government planned to implement a Minerals Resource Rent Tax on iron ore and coal mining.
- The Chinese Government increased rare-earth mineral taxes and established a benchmark rate for a resource tax on coal, gas, oil, and other resources.
- Guinea planned to review all mining contracts in the country and to implement a new mining code, which would increase the Government's equity in mining projects to 33 percent from 15 percent.
- Indonesia planned to set monthly benchmark prices for the export of aluminum, copper, gold, lead, nickel, palladium, platinum, silver, tin, and zinc. In addition, the Government proposed a ministerial decree requiring miners to process raw commodities in the country before export. The Government also planned to issue a decree to ban the export of low-grade thermal coal beginning in 2014.
- Mongolia intended to increase its stake in the Oyu Tolgoi project to 40 percent from its existing 34 percent ownership.

- The Namibian Government planned to increase its involvement in the mining sector through Government-owned mining company Epangelo Mining and refused to commit to a fixed share in future joint ventures.
- Panama intended to pass a law that would allow foreign state-owned companies to participate in Panama's mining sector either by acquiring mining concessions or by establishing joint ventures with companies already operating in the country.
- Peru and Tanzania proposed to increase taxes on mining companies.
- The Peruvian Government revoked Renco Group's mining license to operate the La Oroya smelter.
- South Africa's African National Congress called for resource nationalization and for approval of the country's 26 percent Black Economic Empowerment policy.
- The United States proposed to impose a 5 percent royalty charge on hard rock miners in the United States.
- The Venezuelan Government planned to nationalize gold mines in Venezuela.
- The Venezuelan Government planned to revoke several mining licenses.
- Zimbabwe moved to pass the indigenization law, which establishes that mining companies must surrender as much as a 51 percent ownership in mining operations to indigenous Zimbabweans.

Outlook

Future supply and demand for aluminum, copper, and iron ore are tied mainly to the resolution of the sovereign debt crisis and economic recovery in Europe and demand for commodities in China. Concerns about the European economy have added volatility to the market and have made 2012 price and production estimates difficult to determine. The energy-intensive nature of aluminum production may have an important effect on future production of that metal as European producers may find it hard to compete with production from countries with cheaper energy sources. Competing domestic energy demands in China could also curtail production there, which could lead to an increase in aluminum imports.

Since 2000, China's rapid economic development has resulted in a substantial increase in mineral consumption and consequent increases in the prices for minerals. A recent report by the World Bank and the Development Research Center (a Chinese think tank) suggests that China's economic development has reached a point at which significant changes in its economic model will be necessary. The report calls for a change in emphasis from export-led growth to growth generated from internal consumers and for a reduction in spending for infrastructure and power generation. These changes are projected to reduce China's rate of growth in its GDP by about 2 percent. Such an economic restructuring is expected to change China's consumption of a number of mineral commodities. Consumption of metals could increase at a slower rate, whereas consumption of fertilizers could increase in response to increased incomes and changing diet. Unless one of the other countries undergoing economic development increases its mineral consumption significantly, consumption of some mineral commodities could increase at a slower pace, and prices for those commodities could soften. Other large developing countries, such as Brazil, India, and Russia, are projecting slower rates of economic growth for 2012 than they were forecasting in September 2012. Under such circumstances, cost control could return as the top priority of mining companies (Davis, 2012a, b; Lyons and Davis, 2012).

References Cited

Alpha Natural Resources, Inc., 2011, Alpha Natural Resources acquires Massey Energy Company creating a global leader in metallurgical coal supply: Abingdon, Va., Alpha Natural Resources, Inc. press release, June 1, 2 p.

Apodaca, L.E., 2012, Nitrogen (fixed)—Ammonia: U.S. Geological Survey Mineral Commodity Summaries 2012, p. 112–113.

Barrick Gold Corp., 2011, Barrick offer to Equinox successful—Offer extended: Toronto, Ontario, Canada, Barrick Gold Corp. press release, June 1, 1 p.

Barrick Gold Corp., 2012, Fourth quarter and yearend report 2011: Toronto, Ontario, Canada, Barrick Gold Corp. press release, February 16, 167 p.

Bergin, Tom, 2012, Exxon tempers European shale gas enthusiasm: London, United Kingdom, Thomson Reuters, February 20, accessed July 31, 2012, at *http://uk.reuters.com/article/2012/02/20/exxon-shale-europe-idUKL5E8DK6TJ20120220.*

BP p.l.c., 2012, BP statistical review of world energy June 2012: London United Kingdom, BP p.l.c., June, accessed June 24, 2012, at *http://www.bp.com/liveassets/bp_internet/globalbp/ globalbp_uk_english/reports_and_publications/statistical_energy_review_2011/STAGING/ local_assets/pdf/statistical_review_of_world_energy_full_report_2012.pdf.*

Bray, E.L., 2012a, Aluminum: U.S. Geological Survey Mineral Commodity Summaries 2012, p. 16–17.

Bray, E.L., 2012b, Bauxite and alumina: U.S. Geological Survey Mineral Commodity Summaries 2012, p. 26–27.

Carlin, J.F., Jr., 2012, Tin: U.S. Geological Survey Mineral Commodity Summaries 2012, p. 170–171.

Chen, Sarah, 2012, China forecast soaring shale gas output: The Wall Street Journal, March 16, accessed March 16, 2012, at *http://online.wsj.com/article/SB10001424052702304459804577284743898325490.html.*

Cliffs Natural Resources Inc., 2011a, 2010 annual report: Cleveland, Ohio, Cliffs Natural Resources Inc., 182 p.

Cliffs Natural Resources Inc., 2011b, Cliffs Natural Resources Inc. and Consolidated Thompson Iron Mines announce close of acquisition: Cleveland, Ohio, and Montreal, Quebec, Canada, Cliffs Natural Resources Inc. press release, May 12, 1 p.

Cliffs Natural Resources Inc., 2011c, Form 10–K: U.S. Securities and Exchange Commission, December 31, 199 p.

Cordier, D.J., 2012, Rare earths: U.S. Geological Survey Mineral Commodity Summaries 2012, p. 128–129.

Davenport, Jade, 2011, IFC earmarks $300 m for African mining investments over 3 years: Creamer Media's Mining Weekly, February 9, accessed July 23, 2012, at *http://www.miningweekly.com/ print-version/ifc-earmarks-300m-for-african-mining-investments-over-3-yrs-2011-02-09.*

Davis, Bob, 2012a, China speeds economic 'transformation': The Wall Street Journal, March 6, p. A9.

Davis, Bob, 2012b, World Bank chief urges reforms for Beijing, The Wall Street Journal, February 27, accessed August 28, 2012, at *http://online.wsj.com/article/SB10001424052970204653604577248194277473310.html.*

Deloitte Development LLC, 2011, M&A round-up: New York, N.Y., Deloitte Development LLC, 11 p.

Donville, Christopher, 2011, Minmetals drops Equinox bid after being trumped by Barrick's $7.68 billion: Bloomberg L.P., April 26, accessed March 14, 2012, at *http://www.bloomberg.com/news/2011-04-26/minmetals-withdraws-offer-for-equinox-after-being-outbid-by-barrick-gold.html.*

Edelstein, D.L., 2012, Copper: U.S. Geological Survey Mineral Commodity Summaries 2012, p. 48–49.

Eldorado Gold Corp., 2012, Consolidated financial statements—December 31, 2011 and 2010: Vancouver, British Columbia, Canada, Eldorado Gold Corp., 31 p.

Els, Frink, 2011, Record $8.5 billion likely spent in 2011 exploring for gold: Mining.com, September 18, accessed March 15, 2012, at *http://www.mining.com/2011/09/18/ record-8-5-billion-likely-spent-in-2011-exploring-for-gold/*.

Embassy of the People's Republic of China in the United States of America, 2009, China allocates more than 60 percent of central budget to public works as of May: Beijing, China, Ministry of Foreign Affairs of the People's Republic of China, June 4, accessed March 15, 2012, at *http://www.china-embassy.org/eng/gyzg/t566183.htm*.

Ericsson, Magnus, and Larsson, Viktoriya, 2012, E&MJ's annual survey of global mining investment: Engineering and Mining Journal, v. 213, no. 1, January, p. 24–29, accessed March 14, 2012, at *http://www.e-mj.com/index.php/features/1610-eamjs-annual-survey-of-global-mining-investment.html*.

Ernst & Young, 2011, Business risks facing mining and metals 2011–2012: Ernst & Young, accessed August 28, 2012, at *http://www.ey.com/Publication/vwLUAssets/Business_risks_facing_mining_and_metals_2011-2012/$File/Metal_Mining_paper_02Aug11_lowres.pdf*.

Fathallah, Hadi, 2012, Food security in the Arab World—Global challenges and regional opportunities: Food and Agriculture Organization of the United Nation, *in* Proceedings of 18th AFA Int'l Annual Fertilizer Forum & Exhibition, Sharm El-Sheikh, Egypt, February 7–9, 2012, 16 p.

Fenton, M.D., 2012, Iron and steel: U.S. Geological Survey Mineral Commodity Summaries 2012, p. 78–79.

Fong-Sam, Yolanda, Kuo, C.S., Shi, Lin, Tse, Pui-Kwan, Wacaster, Susan, and Wilburn, D.R., 2012, The mineral industries of Asia and the Pacific, *in* Area reports—International—Asia and the Pacific: U.S. Geological Survey Minerals Yearbook 2010, v. III, p. 1.1–1.19.

George, M.W., 2012, Gold: U.S. Geological Survey Mineral Commodity Summaries 2012, p. 66–67.

Global LNG Ltd., 2012, Global LNG developments in 2010: Global LNG Ltd., accessed August 28, 2012, at *http://www.globallnginfo.com/develop2010.htm*.

Gordon, Julie, 2012, PDAC-Uranium industry warms up after a tough year: Thomson Reuters, March 6, accessed March 16, 2012, at *http://www.reuters.com/article/2012/03/06/ canada-mining-pdac-uranium-idUSL2E8DSF2720120306*.

Heffer, Patrick, and Prud'homme, Michel, 2012, Global supply and demand outlook for fertilizers and raw materials: International Fertilizer Industry Association, *in* Proceedings of 18th AFA Int'l Annual Fertilizer Forum & Exhibition, Sharm El-Sheikh, Egypt, February 7–9, 2012, Presentation, 12 p.

Houssin, Didier, 2012, Medium-term coal market report 2011: International Energy Agency, January 11, 19 p., accessed March 15, 2012, at *http://www.iea.org/speech/2012/houssin_mtcmr.pdf*.

Iliff, Laurence, and Jeffris, Gerald, 2012, Mexico and Brazil fix trade spat over cars: The Wall Street Journal, March 16, accessed August 1, 2012, at *http://online.wsj.com/article/SB10001424052702303863404577284060757942448.html*.

Iosebashvili, Ira, 2012, Russia forecasts slower growth: The Wall Street Journal, April 7–8, p. A8.

Jamasmie, Cecilia, 2012a, Latin America leads global mining exploration spending again: Mining.com, March 5, accessed March 14, 2012, at *http://www.mining.com/2012/03/05/latin-america-leads-global-mining-exploration-spending-again/*.

Jamasmie, Cecilia, 2012b, Peru mining investments reached US $7.2 billion in 2011, 77 percent more than in 2010: Mining.com, March 12, accessed March 14, 2012, at *http://www.mining.com/2012/03/12/peru-mining-investments-reached-us7-2-billion-in-2011-77-more-than-in-2010/.*

Jasinski, S.M., 2012a, Phosphate rock: U.S. Geological Survey Mineral Commodity Summaries 2012, p. 118–119.

Jasinski, S.M., 2012b, Potash: U.S. Geological Survey Mineral Commodity Summaries 2012, p. 122–123.

Jorgenson, J.D., 2012, Iron ore: U.S. Geological Survey Mineral Commodity Summaries 2012, p. 84–85.

KGHM Polska Miedz S.A., 2012, Consolidated quarterly report QSr 4/2011: Lubin, Poland, KGHM Polska Miedz S.A., February 29, 55 p.

Kolyandr, Alexander, 2012, Norway's Statoil signs arctic deal with Russia's Rosneft: The Wall Street Journal, May 7, p. B3.

Kosich, Dorothy, 2010, China to spend $4.48 bn on domestic mining exploration: Mineweb.com, November 8, accessed July 23, 2012, at *http://www.mineweb.com/mineweb/view/mineweb/en/page103118?oid=114427&sn=Detail&pid=102055.*

Loferski, P.J., 2012, Platinum-group metals: U.S. Geological Survey Mineral Commodity Summaries 2012, p. 120–121.

Lyons, John, and Davis, Bob, 2012, Emerging-market engines falter: The Wall Street Journal, March 7, A8.

MacDonald, Alex, 2011, BHP Billiton completed $10 billion share buyback: MarketWatch Inc., June 30, accessed March 14, 2012, at *http://www.marketwatch.com/story/bhp-billiton-completes-10-billion-share-buyback-2011-06-30.*

Maeda, Risa, 2011, Japanese utilities' LNG usage hits record high in August: Tokyo, Japan, Thomson Reuters, September 13, accessed August 1, 2012, at *http://r.einnews.com/BqLaJW.*

Maeda, Risa, 2012a, Japan to restart second reactor amid faultline concerns: Tokyo, Japan, Thomson Reuters, July 18, accessed July 24, 2012, at *http://www.reuters.com/article/2012/07/18/us-japan-nuclear-restart-idUSBRE86H0CO20120718.*

Maeda, Risa, 2012b, Japan utilities Feb LNG consumption rises yr/yr: Thomson Reuters, March 13, accessed August 1, 2012, at *http://www.reuters.com/article/2012/03/13/energy-japan-utilities-idUST9E8DL00320120313.*

Menzie W.D., 2012, Testimony of W. David Menzie, Chief, Global Minerals Analysis Section, National Minerals Information Center, U.S. Geological Survey, U.S. Department of the Interior, before the U.S.-China Economic and Security Review Commission, hearing on "China's global quest for resources and implications for the United States", January 26, 2012: Washington, D.C., U.S.-China Economic and Security Review Commission, 11 p., available at *http://origin.www.uscc.gov/sites/default/files/1.26.12menzie_testimony.pdf.*

Menzie, W.D., Baker, M.S., Bleiwas, D.I., and Kuo, Chin, 2011, Mines and mineral processing facilities in the vicinity of the March 11, 2011, earthquake in northern Honshu, Japan: U.S. Geological Survey Open-File Report 2011–1069, accessed July 19, 2012, at *http://pubs.usgs.gov/of/2011/1069/.*

Metals Economics Group, 2011, Trends in worldwide exploration budgets: Halifax, Nova Scotia, Canada, Metals Economics Group, Strategic Report v. 24, no. 6, 10 p.

Mining Journal, 2011a, Market update: Mining Journal, March 11, 30 p.

Mining Journal, 2011b, Market update: Mining Journal, December 30, 2011/ January 6, 2012, 16 p.

Mishkin, Sarah, 2011, Whiteheaven and Aston in A$4.7 bn merger talks: Hong Kong, China, The Financial Times Ltd., December 5, accessed June 27, 2012, at *http://www.ft.com/intl/cms/s/0/ 564e5da2-1f27-11e1-ab49-00144feabdc0.html#axzz22OW3c29T*.

Mitsubishi Corp., 2011, Acquisition of 24.5 percent of Anglo American Sur, S.A.: Mitsubishi Corp., November 10, accessed March 14, 2012, at *http://www.mitsubishicorp.com/jp/en/pr/archive/ 2011/html/0000013308.html*.

Mobbs, P.M., Taib, Mowafa, Wallace, G.J., Wilburn, D.R., and Yager, T.R., 2012, The mineral industries of the Middle East, *in* Area reports—International—Africa and the Middle East: U.S. Geological Survey Minerals Yearbook 2010, v. III, p. 44.1–44.13.

National Research Council, 2008a, Managing materials for a twenty-first century military: Washington, D.C., The National Academies Press, 190 p.

National Research Council, 2008b, Minerals, critical minerals, and the U.S. economy: Washington, D.C., The National Academies Press, 246 p.

Natural Resources Canada, 2009, Uranium: Natural Resources Canada, accessed July 23, 2012, at *http://www.nrcan.gc.ca/energy/sources/uranium-nuclear/1190*.

Natural Resources Canada, 2012a, Exploration plus deposit appraisal expenditures, by junior and senior companies, by Province and Territory, 2007–2012: Natural Resources Canada, July 23, accessed July 23, 2012, at *http://mmsd.mms.nrcan.gc.ca/stat-stat/expl-expl/6-eng.aspx*.

Natural Resources Canada, 2012b, Exploration plus deposit appraisal expenditures, by Province and Territory, by mineral commodity sought: Natural Resources Canada, July 23, accessed July 23, 2012, at *http://mmsd.mms.nrcan.gc.ca/stat-stat/expl-expl/1-eng.aspx*.

Negishi, Mayumi, and Tsukimori, Osamu, 2012, Inpex to take stake in Shell's Prelude project: Thomson Reuters, March 16, accessed August 1, 2012, at *http://uk.reuters.com/article/2012/03/16/inpex-lng-idUKL4E8EG3NN20120316*.

Newmont Mining Corp., 2011, 2011 annual report and Form 10–K: Greenwood Village, Colo., Newmont Mining Corp., 201 p.

Nicholson, C.V., 2011, Barrick gold to buy Equinox Minerals for $7.8 billion: The New York Times, April 25, accessed March 12, 2013, at *http://dealbook.nytimes.com/2011/04/25/ barrick-to-buy-equinox-minerals-for-7-8-billion/*.

Norsk Hydro ASA, 2011, Hydro-Vale aluminum transaction to be completed today: Oslo, Norway, Norsk Hydro ASA press release, February 28, 3 p.

Olson, D.W., 2012, Diamond (industrial): U.S. Geological Survey Mineral Commodity Summaries 2012, p. 50–51.

Organisation for Economic Co-operation and Development, 2011, Nuclear energy generation and nuclear power plants: Organisation for Economic Co-operation and Development, December 22, accessed July 23, 2012, at *http://www.oecd-ilibrary.org/sites/nuclear-gen-table-2011-1-en/ index.html?contentType=&itemId=/content/table/nuclear-gen-table-2011-1-en&containerItemId=/ content/table/nuclear-gen-table-2011-1-en&accessItemIds=&mimeType=text/html*.

Peabody Energy Inc., 2011, Peabody Energy (NYSE:BTU) completes acquisition of Macarthur Coal: St. Louis, Mo., Peabody Energy Inc. press release, December 20, 2 p.

Peaple, Andrew, 2012, BP maneuvers for a tricky Russian exit: The Wall Street Journal, June 2–3, p. B16.

Perez, A.A., Brininstool, Mark, Safirova, Elena, Anderson, S.T., Newman, H.R., Wallace, G.J., and Wilburn, D.R., 2012, The mineral industries of Europe and Central Eurasia, *in* Area reports— International—Europe and Central Eurasia: U.S. Geological Survey Minerals Yearbook 2010, v. III, p. 1.1–1.37.

PricewaterhouseCoopers LLP, 2012, On the road again?: Toronto, Ontario, Canada, PricewaterhouseCoopers LLP, March, 46 p., accessed March 14, 2012, at *http://www.pwc.com/ en_GX/gx/mining/assets/on-the-road-again-global-mining-2011-deals-review-and-2012-outlook.pdf.*

Rolli, Claudia, 2012, Acordo automotivo com México é positivo, diz Anfavea: Sao Paulo, Brazil, Fohla do Sao Paulo, March 3, accessed March 15, 2012, at *http://www1.folha.uol.com.br/mercado/ 1063173-acordo-automotivo-com-mexico-e-positivo-diz-anfavea.shtml.*

Senior, Anthony, and Huleatt, Mike, 2012, Australian mineral exploration review 2011: Geoscience Australia, February, accessed July 23, 2012, at *https://www.ga.gov.au/products/servlet/controller?event=GEOCAT_DETAILS&catno=73291.*

Sharma, Amol, and Bahree, Megha, 2012, Grinding energy shortage takes toll on India's growth: The Wall Street Journal, July 2, p. A1, A8.

Shiryaevskaya, Anna, 2012, Gazprom trips in India as shale upends Asia gas markets: Bloomberg L.P., March 14, accessed August 1, 2012, at *http://www.bloomberg.com/news/print/2012-03-14/ gazprom-trips-in-india-as-shale-upends-asia-gas-markets-energy.html.*

Swanepoel, Esmarie, 2011, Australian miners invest $20 billion in Africa, 'billions more in the pipeline': Creamer Media's Mining Weekly, August 31, accessed March 15, 2012, at *http://www.miningweekly.com/print-version/australian-miners-invest-20bn-in-africa-billions-more-in-the-pipeline-2011-08-31.*

Thomson Reuters, 2012a, China says found more oil and gas in 2011: Beijing, China, Thomson Reuters, February 23, accessed July 23, 2012, at *http://uk.reuters.com/article/2012/02/23/ china-energy-reserves-idUKL4E8DN3PY20120223.*

Thomson Reuters, 2012b, Iron ore tops Australia's exploration spending list: Sydney, Australia, Thomson Reuters, February 16, accessed July 23, 2012, at *http://www.reuters.com/article/2012/02/17/ mining-australia-spending-idUSL4E8DH03620120217.*

Thomson Reuters, 2012c, Poland may have 1 trillion cubic meters of shale gas: Warsaw, Poland, Thomson Reuters, March 16, accessed August 1, 2012, at *http://www.reuters.com/article/2012/03/16/ poland-shale-idUSL5E8EG3MN20120316.*

Topf, Andrew, 2012, Boart Longyear posts record $2B in sales; forecasts 14 percent growth this year: Mining.com, March 13, accessed March 15, 2012, at *http://www.mining.com/2012/03/13/ boart-longyear-posts-2b-profit-forecasts-14-growth-this-year/.*

Torello, Alessandro, and Robinson, Frances, 2012, Russia curbs supplies of gas across Europe: The Wall Street Journal, February 4–5, p. A11.

U.S. Central Intelligence Agency, 2012, China, in The world factbook: Washington D.C., U.S. Central Intelligence Agency, July 5, accessed March 15, 2012, at *https://www.cia.gov/library/publications/the-world-factbook/geos/ch.html.*

van der Hoeven, Maria, 2012, Global energy trends—Focus on oil & gas: International Energy Agency, February 29, 27 p., accessed March 15, 2012, at *http://www.iea.org/media/mvdh/Mexico_Seminar.pdf.*

Wacaster, Susan, Mobbs, P.M., Wilburn, D.R., Wallace, G.J., Anderson, S.T., Bermúdez-Lugo, Omayra, Gurmendi, A.C., and Perez, A.A., 2012, The mineral industries of Latin America and Canada, *in* Area reports—International—Latin America and Canada: U.S. Geological Survey Minerals Yearbook 2010, v., p. 1.1–1.22.

Whitehaven Coal Ltd., 2012, Letter from the chairman: Whitehaven Coal Ltd., March 14, 26 p.

Wilburn, D.R., Rapstine, T.D., and Lee, E.C., 2012, Exploration review: Mining Engineering, v. 64, no. 5, May, 40–60 p.

World Nuclear Association, 2012, Nuclear power in France: World Nuclear Association, June, accessed March 16, 2012, at *http://www.world-nuclear.org/info/inf40.html.*

Yager, T.R., Bermúdez-Lugo, Omayra, Mobbs, P.M., Newman, H.R., Taib, Mowafa, Wallace, G.J., and
Wilburn, D.R., 2012, The mineral industries of Africa, *in* Area reports—International—Africa and the
Middle East: U.S. Geological Survey Minerals Yearbook 2010, v. III, p. 1.1–1.24.

Yep, Eric, 2012, Power problems threaten growth in India: The Wall Street Journal, January 3, p. A11.

Table 1. Historic and projected bauxite mine production, 2000–2017.[1]

[Gross weight in thousand metric tons]

Country	2000	2005	2010	2013e	2015e	2017e
Australia	53,800	59,960	68,414	80,000	85,000	91,000
Brazil	13,800	22,034	31,700	32,000	32,000	32,000
China	9,000	22,000	44,000	46,000	47,000	48,000
Guinea	15,700	14,600	15,100	15,000	27,000	37,000
India	7,560	12,385	18,000	21,000	23,000	25,000
Indonesia	1,150	1,442	1,050	6,000	12,000	20,000
Jamaica	11,100	14,116	8,540	11,000	11,000	11,000
Kazakhstan	3,729	4,800	5,310	5,500	5,500	5,500
Russia	5,274	6,400	5,475	5,500	5,550	5,600
Saudi Arabia[2]	--	--	--	--	3,500	4,000
Sierra Leone	--	--	1,090	1,100	6,100	11,100
Suriname	3,610	4,757	4,000	5,000	5,000	5,000
Venezuela	4,360	5,900	5,500	5,500	5,500	5,000
Others	8,260	8,850	7,340	10,800	11,200	11,300
World	137,000	177,000	216,000	244,000	279,000	312,000

[e]Estimated. -- Negligible or no production.

[1]Estimated data and totals are rounded to no more than three significant digits; may not add to totals shown.

[2]Does not include production of low-grade bauxite for cement, which began in 2008.

Table 2. Historic and projected primary and secondary aluminum metal production, 2000–2017.[1]

[Thousand metric tons]

Country	2000	2005	2010	2013[e]	2015[e]	2017[e]
Australia	1,770	2,030	1,928	2,000	2,050	2,100
Bahrain[2]	509	751	851	870	870	870
Brazil	1,487	1,749	1,787	2,000	2,500	2,500
Canada[3]	2,521	3,070	3,000	3,600	3,900	3,900
China	2,800	9,740	20,200	23,000	25,000	27,000
Germany	1,216	1,366	1,014	1,000	1,000	1,000
Iceland	224	273	813	815	815	815
India	644	942	1,450	1,800	2,000	2,200
Iran	140	220	270	600	823	823
Italy	848	1,314	1,414	1,500	1,500	1,500
Norway	1,280	1,376	1,100[e]	1,200	1,200	1,200
Russia	3,245	3,647	3,947	4,000	4,200	4,400
South Africa	673	846	807	810	810	810
United Arab Emirates	470	722	1,400	2,400	2,400	2,400
United States	5,038	3,030	2,800	3,200	3,200	3,200
Others	7,792	8,733	7,858	10,000	11,000	11,000
World	31,000	40,000	51,000	59,000	63,000	66,000

[e]Estimated.

[1]Estimated data and totals are rounded to no more than three significant digits; may not add to totals shown.

[2]May include some secondary aluminum produced from used beverage cans.

[3]Includes secondary aluminum production.

Table 3. Historic and projected cobalt mine production, 2000–2017.[1]

[Metal content in metric tons]

Country	2000	2005	2010	2013e	2015e	2017e
Australia	5,600	5,600	3,850	4,000	4,000	4,000
Botswana	300	326	340	350	350	350
Brazil	900	1,500	1,500	1,500	1,500	1,500
Canada	5,298	5,767	4,568	7,000	9,000	9,000
China	90	2,100	6,000	6,000	6,000	6,000
Congo (Kinshasa)	10,000	24,500	61,000	95,700	105,000	116,000
Cuba	2,800	4,800	3,600	3,600	4,400	4,400
Indonesia	--	1,600	1,600	1,300	1,100	1,100
Kazakhstan	300	--	--	--	--	--
Madagascar	--	--	700	4,900	5,600	5,600
Morocco	1,300	1,600	3,130	3,200	3,200	3,200
New Caledonia	1,700	1,800	1,700	1,000	4,000	5,000
Papua New Guinea	--	--	--	1,500	3,000	3,000
Philippines	--	300	2,200	2,500	5,000	5,000
Russia	4,000	6,300	6,200	6,200	6,200	6,200
South Africa	580	620	400	1,000	1,000	1,000
Zambia	4,600	9,300	5,700	7,000	7,000	7,000
Zimbabwe	79	281	60	200	200	200
World	37,000	66,000	103,000	147,000	167,000	179,000

eEstimated. -- Negligible or no production.

[1]Estimated data and totals are rounded to no more than three significant digits; may not add to totals shown.

Table 4. Historic and projected copper mine production, 2000–2017.[1]

[Metal content in thousand metric tons]

Country	2000	2005	2010	2013e	2015e	2017e
Argentina	145	187	140	200	300	300
Australia	829	930	870	1,100	1,200	1,250
Brazil	32	133	214	240	250	260
Bulgaria	92	112	110	110	110	110
Canada	634	595	525	640	640	650
Chile	4,602	5,321	5,419	5,700	5,900	6,000
China	593	762	1,160	1,300	1,400	1,450
Congo (Kinshasa)	31	97	440	777	950	990
Indonesia	1,010	1,064	878	900	1,000	1,100
Iran	125	190	255	350	350	400
Kazakhstan	430	402	380	400	480	520
Mexico	365	429	238	320	350	350
Mongolia	125	127	125	200	400	800
Papua New Guinea	203	193	160	120	150	245
Peru	554	1,010	1,094	1,350	1,400	1,450
Poland	509	575	481	500	500	500
Russia	570	640	703	720	740	760
South Africa	137	89	103	106	106	106
United States	1,450	1,140	1,110	1,110	1,110	1,110
Zambia	249	447	820	900	1,000	1,600
Others	693	611	644	800	800	850
World	13,000	15,000	16,000	18,000	19,000	21,000

eEstimated.

[1]Estimated data and totals are rounded to no more than three significant digits; may not add to totals shown.

Table 5. Historic and projected refined copper metal production, 2000–2017.[1]

[Thousand metric tons]

Country	2000	2005	2010	2013e	2015e	2017e
Australia	488	461	417	500	500	500
Belgium	423	382	370	500	500	500
Brazil	233	224	233	250	260	270
Canada	613	515	319	370	370	370
Chile[2]	2,668	2,824	3,244	3,400	3,400	3,400
China	1,370	2,600	4,650	5,300	5,600	5,800
Congo (Kinshasa)	--	--	262	655	855	899
Germany	710	638	704	700	700	700
India	243	497	720	740	750	760
Indonesia	158	263	280	350	360	360
Iran	156	178	210	440	440	700
Japan	1,440	1,395	1,549	1,600	1,600	1,600
Kazakhstan	395	388	323	420	500	520
Korea, Republic of	468	519	541	540	550	600
Mexico	411	416	278	360	390	390
Peru[2]	452	512	394	450	500	550
Poland	486	560	547	600	600	600
Russia	840	933	874	890	906	920
Spain	316	302	290	310	320	330
United States	1,790	1,260	1,098	1,100	1,100	1,100
Zambia	227	399	530	600	600	600
Others	1,091	1,261	1,347	1,500	1,500	1,500
World	15,000	16,000	19,000	22,000	22,000	23,000

eEstimated. -- Negligible or no production.

[1]Estimated data and totals are rounded to no more than three significant digits; may not add to totals shown.

[2]Primary only

Table 6. Historic and projected gold mine production, 2000–2017.[1]

[Metal content in kilograms]

Country	2000	2005	2010	2013[e]	2015[e]	2017[e]
Argentina	26,000	27,904	63,138	60,000	60,000	60,000
Australia	269,000	263,000	261,000	280,000	300,000	320,000
Brazil	50,400	38,293	62,047	65,000	65,500	66,000
Burkina Faso[2]	625	1,397	24,104	28,900	39,300	42,500
Canada	156,200	120,541	91,024	105,000	100,000	110,000
Chile	54,100	40,447	39,494	45,000	60,000	70,000
China	180,000	225,000	345,000	370,000	390,000	400,000
Colombia	37,000	35,783	53,600	55,000	55,000	55,000
Congo (Kinshasa)	69	7,200	3,500	8,000	23,800	26,100
Dominican Republic	--	--	--	25,000	25,000	25,000
Ghana[2]	72,080	66,852	76,332	87,800	103,000	106,000
Indonesia	125,000	130,620	106,316	120,000	130,000	140,000
Kazakhstan	28,171	18,062	30,272	40,000	50,000	70,000
Mali[2]	28,717	44,230	36,344	49,500	49,700	45,600
Mauritania	--	--	8,300	10,500	49,000	49,000
Mexico	26,400	30,356	72,600	75,000	80,000	80,000
Mongolia	11,800	24,120	6,000	13,500	23,500	28,500
Papua New Guinea	74,500	68,483	62,900	62,000	69,000	131,000
Peru	139,000	208,002	164,060	170,000	180,000	185,000
Philippines	36,540	37,490	40,847	43,000	45,000	47,000
Russia	142,738	163,186	189,000	200,000	205,000	210,000
South Africa	430,800	294,671	188,701	221,000	228,000	223,000
Sudan	5,774	3,625	26,317	31,600	32,500	29,700
Tanzania	15,060	47,270	39,448	48,600	51,600	56,300
Turkey	500	4,170	17,000	30,000	40,000	40,000
United States	353,000	256,000	231,000	230,000	230,000	230,000
Uzbekistan	85,000	84,210	90,000	91,000	92,000	93,000
Others	196,000	220,000	236,000	274,000	307,000	316,000
World	2,540,000	2,460,000	2,560,000	2,840,000	3,080,000	3,250,000

[e]Estimated. -- Negligible or no production.

[1]Estimated data and totals are rounded to no more than three significant digits; may not add to totals shown.

[2]Excludes production from artisanal mining.

Table 7. Historic and projected beneficiated iron ore production, 2000–2017.[1]

[Metal content in thousand metric tons]

Country	Average ore grade (% Fe)	2000	2005	2010	2013[e]	2015[e]	2017[e]
Australia	62	107,000	163,000	271,000	330,000	350,000	370,000
Brazil	66	141,000	186,891	247,772	250,000	250,000	260,000
Canada[2]	64	22,700	19,333	23,300	28,000	28,000	30,000
Chile	61	5,400	4,707	5,852	7,000	8,000	9,000
China	64	73,600	134,000	350,000	410,000	420,000	430,000
Gabon	64	--	--	--	640	3,200	12,800
Guinea	30 to 68	--	--	--	7,100	103,000	119,000
India	64	48,600	97,500	166,000	170,000	172,000	174,000
Iran	-	5,800	9,162	16,500	30,000	30,000	35,000
Kazakhstan	57	9,200	11,100	13,800 [e]	15,000	17,000	17,000
Mauritania	59 to 72	7,500	7,000	7,500	8,500	10,000	10,000
Mexico	60	6,800	7,012	7,900	8,000	8,500	8,500
Peru	68	2,810	4,565	6,140	6,500	7,000	7,000
Russia	58	50,000	56,100	58,500	59,000	59,500	60,000
Saudi Arabia	-	--	--	--	--	500	4,700
Senegal	42 to 59	--	--	--	--	--	4,350
Sierra Leone	66	--	--	--	9,360	10,100	10,100
South Africa	62 to 65	21,570	24,900	36,900	46,700	48,900	49,500
Sweden	65	13,556	15,300	16,750	16,000	16,000	15,000
Ukraine	55	30,600	37,700	43,000	45,000	48,000	50,000
United States	-	39,703	34,202	32,000	32,000	32,000	32,000
Venezuela	65	11,100	13,000	15,200	16,000	16,500	16,500
Other	-	10,402	11,272	16,370	21,400	23,400	26,000
World	-	607,000	837,000	1,320,000	1,520,000	1,660,000	1,750,000

[e]Estimated. -- Negligible or no production.

[1]Estimated data and totals are rounded to no more than three significant digits; may not add to totals shown.

[2]Includes beneficiated and direct-shipping ore.

Table 8. Historic and projected crude steel production, 2000–2017.[1]

[Thousand metric tons]

Country	2000	2005	2010	2013[e]	2015[e]	2017[e]
Brazil	27,900	31,631	33,033	34,000	35,000	40,000
Canada	15,900	15,327	13,003	13,000	15,000	15,000
China	129,000	353,240	637,230	730,000	750,000	780,000
France	21,002	19,481	15,414	17,000	18,000	18,000
Germany	46,376	44,524	43,830	45,000	45,000	45,000
India	26,900	45,800	66,800	72,000	74,000	76,000
Iran	6,600	9,400	12,000	18,000	30,000	35,000
Italy	26,544	29,061	25,750	28,000	30,000	30,000
Japan	106,400	112,470	110,000	115,000	118,000	120,000
Korea, Republic of	43,100	47,820	58,912	59,000	61,000	60,000
Mexico	15,600	16,202	16,710	17,000	19,000	20,000
Poland	10,508	8,336	7,996	9,000	10,000	10,000
Russia	59,097	66,186	66,300	66,400	66,500	66,600
Spain	15,844	17,800	16,311	16,500	17,000	17,000
Taiwan	17,300	18,567	20,498	23,000	23,000	23,000
Turkey	14,325	20,960	29,030	35,000	43,000	43,000
Ukraine	31,780	38,636	33,599	40,000	43,000	48,000
United Kingdom	15,306	13,210	9,709	13,000	13,000	13,000
United States	102,000	94,900	80,500	92,000	92,000	92,000
Others	116,877	140,072	136,880	160,000	170,000	173,000
World	848,000	1,140,000	1,430,000	1,600,000	1,670,000	1,720,000

[e]Estimated.

[1]Estimated data and totals are rounded to no more than three significant digits; may not add to totals shown.

Table 9. Historic and projected palladium mine production, 2000–2017.[1]

[Metal content in kilograms]

Country	2000	2005	2010	2013e	2015e	2017e
Australia	812	550	650	650	700	700
Canada	10,400	10,400	6,200	15,000	15,000	19,000
China	350	450	650	650	700	700
Russia	95,000	97,400	84,700	85,000	85,000	85,000
South Africa	55,818	82,961	82,222	97,200	106,000	108,000
United States	10,300	13,300	11,600	12,000	12,000	12,000
Zimbabwe	366	3,879	7,000	9,000	11,000	11,000
Other	33	29	37	35	35	35
World	173,000	209,000	193,000	220,000	230,000	236,000

eEstimated.

[1]Estimated data and totals are rounded to no more than three significant digits; may not add to totals shown.

Table 10. Historic and projected platinum mine production, 2000–2017.[1]

[Metal content in kilograms]

Country	2000	2005	2010	2013e	2015e	2017e
Australia	171	111	130	200	200	200
Canada	5,700	6,075	3,600	9,000	9,000	10,000
China	650	700	750	1,000	1,000	1,000
Colombia	339	1,082	997	1,200	1,200	1,200
Finland	441	678	275	200	200	200
Russia	27,000	29,000	25,000	26,000	26,000	26,000
South Africa	114,459	163,711	147,790	174,000	188,000	193,000
United States	3,110	3,920	3,450	3,500	3,500	3,500
Zimbabwe	505	4,834	8,800	11,000	12,000	13,000
Others	1,024	23	33	25	25	25
World	153,000	210,000	191,000	226,000	241,000	248,000

eEstimated.

[1]Estimated data and totals are rounded to no more than three significant digits; may not add to totals shown.

Table 11. Historic and projected tin mine production, 2000–2017.[1]

[Metal content in metric tons]

Country	2000	2005	2010	2013[e]	2015[e]	2017[e]
Australia	9,146	2,819	7,000	6,000	6,000	6,000
Bolivia	12,293	18,640	20,190	20,000	23,000	24,000
Brazil	14,200	11,739	10,400	12,000	14,000	14,500
China	99,400	126,000	115,000	120,000	110,000	110,000
Congo (Kinshasa)	50	4,400	6,300	4,000	4,000	4,000
Egypt	--	--	--	1,530	1,530	1,530
Indonesia	55,624	78,404	43,258	45,000	44,000	42,000
Malaysia	6,307	2,857	2,668	2,500	2,500	2,500
Peru	70,901	42,145	33,848	41,000	42,000	42,500
Rwanda	276	170	1,400	1,500	1,500	1,500
Vietnam	1,800	5,400	5,400	5,400	5,400	5,400
Others	9,123	6,260	1,739	1,700	1,900	2,000
World	279,000	299,000	247,000	261,000	256,000	256,000

[e]Estimated. -- Negligible or no production.

[1]Estimated data and totals are rounded to no more than three significant digits; may not add to totals shown.

Table 12. Historic and projected tin metal production, 2000–2017.[1]

[Metric tons]

Country	2000	2005	2010	2013[e]	2015[e]	2017[e]
Australia	1,033	994	3,400	2,000	2,000	2,000
Bolivia	9,353	13,841	14,975	17,000	20,000	21,000
Brazil	14,023	9,236	9,348	10,500	12,000	12,000
China	112,000	122,000	150,000	165,000	170,000	180,000
Indonesia	47,129	65,300	43,832	45,000	50,000	55,000
Malaysia	26,228	36,924	38,737	40,000	40,000	40,000
Peru	37,410	36,733	36,451	39,500	40,000	40,000
Thailand	17,076	31,600	19,423	20,000	23,500	30,000
Others	10,448	9,916	4,341	4,400	5,000	5,000
World	275,000	326,000	321,000	343,000	362,000	385,000

[e]Estimated.

[1]Estimated data and totals are rounded to no more than three significant digits; may not add to totals shown.

Table 13. Historic and projected diamond production, 2000–2017.[1]

[Thousand carats]

Country	2000	2005	2010	2013[e]	2015[e]	2017[e]
Angola	4,313	7,079	13,000	10,000	10,000	10,000
Australia	26,600	34,307	10,000	11,000	11,000	11,000
Botswana	24,635	31,890	21,000	28,000	28,000	28,000
Canada	2,530	12,314	11,773	12,000	13,000	16,000
Congo (Kinshasa)	16,006	35,207	16,800	19,500	19,500	19,500
Ghana	878	1,013	334	300	900	900
Namibia	1,552	1,902	1,693	1,800	2,000	2,000
Russia	29,200	38,000	32,800	33,000	33,000	33,000
Sierra Leone	77	669	438	500	500	500
South Africa	10,790	15,776	8,868	8,200	8,500	9,100
Tanzania	354	220	80	510	640	640
Zimbabwe	23	251	8,435	10,000	11,000	10,000
Other	4,363	2,205	1,871	2,200	2,200	2,300
World	121,000	181,000	127,000	137,000	140,000	143,000

[e]Estimated.

[1]Estimated data and totals are rounded to no more than three significant digits; may not add to totals shown.

Table 14. Historic and projected lithium production, 2000–2017.[1]

[Metal content in metric tons]

Country	2000	2005	2010	2013[e]	2015[e]	2017[e]
Argentina	25	2,800	2,100	2,800	2,800	2,800
Australia	2,300	4,800	8,200	10,000	15,000	15,000
Bolivia	--	--	--	--	50	90
Brazil	260	210	489	510	510	510
Canada	670	670	--	2,000	3,000	3,000
Chile	6,740	8,354	10,361	13,000	13,000	13,000
China	3,000	3,600	5,100	5,200	5,300	5,300
Portugal	--	520	810	820	830	870
United States	W	W	W	W	W	W
Zimbabwe	1,100	1,100	700	800	800	800
World	14,000	22,000	28,000	35,000	41,000	41,000

[e]Estimated. -- Negligible or no production. W Withheld to avoid disclosing company proprietary data; not included in "World."

[1]Estimated data and totals are rounded to no more than three significant digits; may not add to totals shown.

Table 15.   Historic and projected salable coal production, 2000–2017.[1]

[Thousand metric tons]

Country	2000	2005	2010	2013e	2015e	2017e
Australia	313,000	370,000	499,000	530,000	540,000	560,000
Canada[2]	69,200	67,555	67,876	70,000	75,000	80,000
China	957,000	2,260,000	3,240,000	3,500,000	3,700,000	3,900,000
Colombia	38,200	59,064	74,350	85,000	85,000	100,000
Czech Republic	68,091	61,903	55,124	56,000	56,000	56,000
Germany	201,975	202,815	182,303	177,000	175,000	172,000
Greece	64,026	73,585	64,000	65,000	65,000	65,000
India	335,000	360,000	507,000	510,000	520,000	530,000
Indonesia	102,015	192,920	256,789	270,000	273,000	275,000
Kazakhstan	74,872	86,385	106,568	110,000	120,000	130,000
Korea, North	22,500	23,500	41,000	40,000	40,000	40,000
Mexico[2]	14,300	11,750	27,565	30,000	32,000	32,000
Mongolia	5,185	8,256	25,246	30,000	30,000	30,000
Mozambique	16	3	50	15,700	31,000	42,000
Poland	162,815	159,039	133,238	135,000	135,000	135,000
Romania	29,294	34,201	30,000	30,000	30,000	30,000
Russia	273,578	298,300	326,050	330,000	335,000	340,000
Serbia[3]	32,275	34,993	38,598	38,000	38,000	38,000
South Africa	224,118	244,940	254,522	293,000	330,000	351,000
Turkey	64,645	58,676	78,104	80,000	90,000	90,000
Ukraine	81,907	74,559	75,200	80,000	85,000	90,000
United States	974,118	1,028,538	983,188	1,000,000	1,000,000	1,000,000
Vietnam	11,609	34,093	44,011	50,000	50,000	50,000
Others	185,000	172,000	176,000	186,000	192,000	196,000
World	4,120,000	5,920,000	7,290,000	7,710,000	8,030,000	8,330,000

eEstimated.

[1]Estimated data and totals are rounded to no more than three significant digits; may not add to totals shown.

[2]Run of mine.

[3]Prior to 2005, figures are for a combined Serbia (including Kosovo) and Montenegro.